This is one of a series of books on modern art created to help very young people learn the basic vocabulary used by artists, a sort of ABC of art. Parents and teachers play a key role in this learning process, encouraging careful, thoughtful looking. The book isolates lines to show how they are used by artists and how they contribute to meaning in art. By looking at lines and discussing what thoughts and feelings they convey, adults encourage children to develop creative thinking skills. At the back of this book, there is more information about the pictures to help in this engaging process.

Enjoy looking together!

Lines

Philip Yenawine

Lines

The Museum of Modern Art, New York

Permissions and copyright notices:
Page 1: © 2006 Estate of Pablo Picasso/Artists Rights Society (ARS), New York
Page 2: © Succession Miró/Artists Rights Society (ARS), New York/ ADAGP, Paris
Page 5: © 2006 Artists Rights Society (ARS), New York/VG Bild-Kunst, Bonn
Pages 8, 16: © 2006 Succession H. Matisse, Paris/Artists Rights Society (ARS), New York
Page 9: © 2006 The Georgia O'Keeffe Foundation/Artists Rights Society (ARS), New York
Page 10: © 2006 Pollock-Krasner Foundation/Artists Rights Society (ARS), New York
Pages 12, 18: © 2006 Artists Rights Society (ARS), New York/ADAGP, Paris

Second edition 1999
Third edition 2006

Library of Congress Control Number: 2006924454
ISBN: 978-0-87070-175-7

Published by The Museum of Modern Art
11 West 53 Street
New York, New York 10019
(www.moma.org)

Distributed in the United States and Canada by D.A.P., Distributed Art Publishers, Inc., New York.

Distributed outside the United States and Canada by Thames & Hudson Ltd., London

Front cover: Detail of Vasily Kandinsky, *Watercolor (Number 13)*. 1913.
Watercolor on paper, 12 $^5/_8$ x 16 $^1/_8$" (32.1 x 41 cm).
Katherine S. Dreier Bequest

Printed in China

Artists make pictures out of lines.

Pablo Picasso. *The Kitchen*

Lines start with a dot •
And a dot grows into a line ••••••••••▬▬
And the lines form shapes.
Find dots. And lines. And shapes.

Joan Miró. Plate 2 from the *Black and Red Series*

Here's a picture made only from lines crossing over one another.
Look very carefully.

Giorgio Morandi. *Large Still Life with Coffeepot*

Some lines are straight.

Some curve.

Some zigzag.

Some loop.

Some make shapes.

Can you find curving lines and straight ones, loops and zigzags?
What shapes can you find?

Paul Klee. *Twittering Machine*

Of course, lines can be any color.

Franz Marc. *Blue Horse with Rainbow*

And there are many ways to make them.
Brushes   Pens   Crayons   Pencils   Fingers

Some lines are thin.

Henri Matisse. *The Swan,* from *Poèsies* by Stéphane Mallarmé

Some are thick.

Lines can sparkle and wiggle.

Jackson Pollock. *One: Number 31, 1950*

Detail of Pollock, *One: Number 31, 1950*

Lines can help us imagine things.

Vasily Kandinsky. *Watercolor (Number 13)*

Can you imagine clouds?

A boat?

Smoke?

Can you find a line moving fast?

Moving slowly?

What else can you find?

Artists draw what they see.

Theo van Doesburg (Christian Emil Marie Küpper). *Composition (The Cow)* and *Study for Composition (The Cow)*

But then they can change things.
Do you see how the cow changes?

Theo van Doesburg (Christian Emil Marie Küpper). Two drawings for *Composition (The Cow)*

Artists draw outlines of shapes we know.
Find people and pictures
and plants and chairs.

Henri Matisse. *The Red Studio*

But not all the lines outline shapes.
How many other places can you see lines?

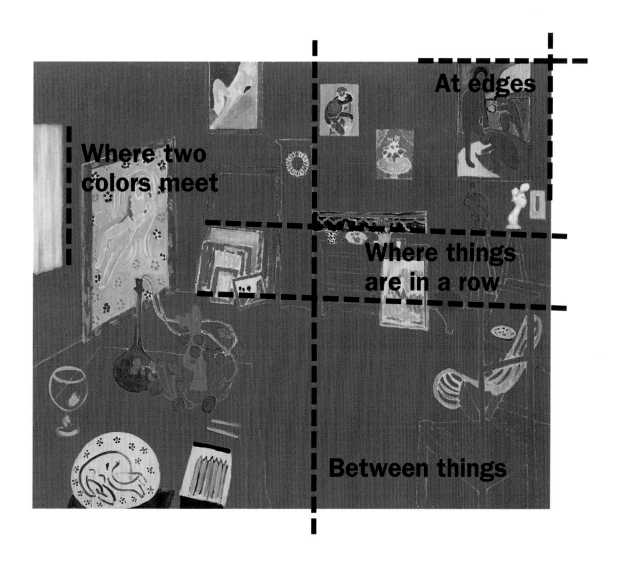

At edges

Where two colors meet

Where things are in a row

Between things

This picture has lines that you will find if you look carefully.

André Derain. *London Bridge*

Can you find:

A line of yellow light flashing on the green water?

Lines of swirling water beneath the bridge?

A line of traffic on the bridge?

How do you think you would feel walking across this bridge?

This painting is made up of tiny lines of color.

Vincent van Gogh. *The Starry Night*

Lines make all sorts of shapes. Find these:

They tell a story about a very bright and starry night in a small village. Can you tell the rest of the story?

Can you draw a picture with thick lines and thin lines, with curves and colors, with shapes we know? With lines to make us imagine?

The art in this book can be found at The Museum of Modern Art in New York City. Other museums and galleries have many interesting pictures too, and it is good to make a habit of visiting them, looking for lines. You can also look in magazines, books, buildings, parks, and gardens.

Page 1
Pablo Picasso
The Kitchen. 1948
Oil on canvas
69" x 8' 2 ½" (175.3 x 250 cm)
Acquired through the Nelson A. Rockefeller Bequest

Widely admired for inventing new systems for composing pictures, Picasso never abandoned images that relate, somehow, to the real world. This is an abstracted representation of Picasso's kitchen as seen from his studio window.

Page 2
Joan Miró
Plate 2 from the *Black and Red Series*
1983
Etching, printed in black
Composition: 6 ⁵/₈ x 10 ³/₁₆" (16.8 x 25.8 cm); plate: 6 ⁵/₈ x 10 ½" (16.9 x 26.7 cm); sheet: 12 ¹⁵/₁₆ x 17 ⁵/₈" (32.9 x 44.8 cm)
Purchased with the Frances Keech Fund and funds given by Agnes Gund and Daniel Shapiro, Gilbert Kaplan, Jeanne C. Thayer, Reba and Dave Williams, Lee and Ann Fensterstock, Linda Barth Goldstein, Walter Bareiss, Mrs. Melville Wakeman Hall, Emily Rauh Pulitzer, and Mr. and Mrs. Herbert D. Schimmel

Miró's form of Surrealism had particularly playful qualities. He freed himself from the impulse to draw realistically. Help children find people and things in this print, letting their imaginations work alongside their logic.

Page 3
Giorgio Morandi
Large Still Life with Coffeepot. 1933, half the edition printed 1943, the other half printed 1949
Etching
Plate: 11 ¹¹/₁₆ x 15 ³/₈" (29.7 x 39 cm); sheet: 15 ¹/₁₆ x 20 ⅛" (38.3 x 51.1 cm)
Mrs. Bertram Smith Fund

The quiet, timeless quality in this still life by Morandi derives partly from the slow, painstaking construction of images by cross-hatching lines.

Page 5
Paul Klee
Twittering Machine. 1922
Watercolor, transfer drawing, and ink on paper mounted on board with gouache and ink additions
25 ¼ x 19" (63.8 x 48.1 cm)
Purchase

Klee's work is valued in part for his playful images and his equally free use of materials and techniques. Children are likely to be amused by the thought of Klee's funny "birds" twittering while they work.

Page 6
Franz Marc
Blue Horse with Rainbow. 1913
Watercolor, gouache, and pencil on paper
6 ³/₈ x 10 ⅛" (16.2 x 25.7 cm)
John S. Newberry Collection

Franz Marc sought expression of the spirit through colors and the use of the horse as a symbol for freedom and strength.

Page 8
Henri Matisse
The Swan, from *Poèsies* by Stéphane
Mallarmé. 1930–32
Etching
Page: 12 ¹⁵/₁₆ x 9 ¹³/₁₆" (33 x 25 cm)
The Louis E. Stern Collection

Always striving to perfect his drawing
skills, Matisse developed the capacity to
describe objects with a sure and simple
line while also maintaining an eye for over-
all design.

Page 9
Georgia O'Keeffe
Evening Star, No. III. 1917
Watercolor on paper mounted on board
8 ⁷/₈ x 11 ⁷/₈" (22.7 x 30.4 cm)
Mr. and Mrs. Donald B. Straus Fund

O'Keeffe specialized in looking closely at
nature and representing its phenomena—
such as sunsets—somewhat abstractly
and rich in color.

Page 10
Jackson Pollock
One: Number 31, 1950. 1950
Oil and enamel on unprimed canvas
8' 10" x 17' 5 ⁵/₈" (269.5 x 530.8 cm)
Sidney and Harriet Janis Collection Fund
(by exchange)

Pollock's painting technique replaced
careful brushwork with athletic action. He
poured, dripped, and cast huge networks
of lines and colors that flickered with light,
encapsulating the energy of America at
midcentury.

Page 12
Vasily Kandinsky
Watercolor (Number 13). 1913
Watercolor on paper
12 ⁵/₈ x 16 ¹/₈" (32.1 x 41 cm)
Katherine S. Dreier Bequest

Kandinsky was interested in conveying
the spiritual side of nature by representing
it in organic rhythms of line and color.

Page 14
Theo van Doesburg
(Christian Emil Marie Küpper)
Composition (The Cow). c. 1917
Pencil on paper
4 ⁵/₈ x 6 ¹/₄" (11.7 x 15.9 cm)
Purchase

Simplifying is an aspect of abstraction,
and here van Doesburg reduced a drawing of an actual cow into geometric
shapes, finally depicting the idea of a
cow, stolid and blocky.

Page 14
Theo van Doesburg
(Christian Emil Marie Küpper)
Study for Composition (The Cow). 1917
Pencil on paper
4 ¹/₈ x 5 ³/₄" (10.4 x 14.6 cm)
Gift of Nelly van Doesburg

Page 15
Theo van Doesburg
(Christian Emil Marie Küpper)
Composition (The Cow). c. 1917
Pencil on paper
4 ⁵/₈ x 6 ¹/₄" (11.7 x 15.9 cm)
Purchase

Page 15
Theo van Doesburg
(Christian Emil Marie Küpper)
Composition (The Cow). c. 1917
Pencil on paper
4 ⁵/₈ x 6 ¹/₄" (11.7 x 15.9 cm)
Purchase

Page 16
Henri Matisse
The Red Studio. 1911
Oil on canvas
71 ¼" x 7' 2 ¼" (181 x 219.1 cm)
Mrs. Simon Guggenheim Fund

Matisse's interest in color could be the main subject of this painting. The color red dominates the work, subverting our spatial expectations and invading the outlined objects.

Page 18
André Derain
London Bridge. 1906
Oil on canvas
26 x 39" (66 x 99.1 cm)
Gift of Mr. and Mrs. Charles Zadok

Derain was primarily interested in representing the world in flashing, brilliant colors, leaving expressive evidence of his brush in marks as energetic and passionate as the colors.

Page 20
Vincent van Gogh
The Starry Night. 1889
Oil on canvas
29 x 36 ¼" (73.7 x 92.1 cm)
Acquired through the Lillie P. Bliss Bequest

This work combines subject, color, and line to create an emotion-charged night sky, filled with awe and perhaps some fright.